HOW ARE ANIMALS GROUPED?

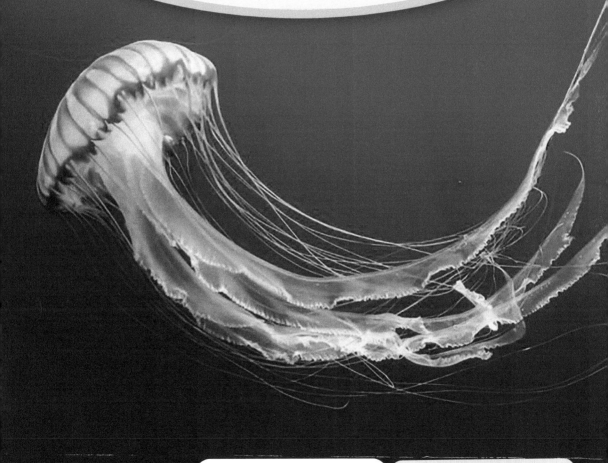

by Lisa M. Bolt Simons

PEBBLE

a capstone imprint

T0084507

Pebble Explore is published by Pebble, an imprint of Capstone.
1710 Roe Crest Drive
North Mankato, Minnesota 56003
www.capstonepub.com

Library of Congress Cataloging-in-Publication Data
Names: Simons, Lisa M. B., 1969- author.
Title: How are animals grouped? / Lisa M. Bolt Simons.
Description: North Mankato, Minnesota : Pebble, [2022] | Series: Science inquiry | Includes bibliographical references and index. | Audience: Ages 5-8 | Audience: Grades 2-3 | Summary: "Bald eagles, bees, and bats all fly. But a bee is an insect. A bat is a mammal. And a bald eagle is a bird! Why are these animals sorted into different groups? Let's investigate animal classification!"— Provided by publisher.
Identifiers: LCCN 2021002875 (print) | LCCN 2021002876 (ebook) | ISBN 9781977131386 (hardcover) | ISBN 9781977132550 (paperback) | ISBN 9781977154347 (pdf) | ISBN 9781977156013 (kindle edition)
Subjects: LCSH: Animals—Classification—Juvenile literature.
Classification: LCC QL351 .S498 2022 (print) | LCC QL351 (ebook) | DDC 590.1/2—dc23
LC record available at https://lccn.loc.gov/2021002875
LC ebook record available at https://lccn.loc.gov/2021002876

Image Credits
iStockphoto/Eraxion, 25; Shutterstock: aaltair, 7 (sea star), Alexey Seafarer, 7 (polar bear), Andrey Pavlov, 7 (ant), Andrey Snider-Bell, 27, AnujinM, 7 (deer), Beatrice Prezzemoli, 14, bebek_moto, 16, bogdan ionescu, 7 (salamander), Butterfly Hunter, 7 (butterfly), cwieders, 13, Damsea, 29, Darryl Vest, 22, Dirk Ercken, 15, DWI YULIANTO, cover (bottom left), Elnur, 11, Eric Isselee, 7 (frog, peacock, snake), F.Rubion, 17, fivespots, 7 (turtle), FloridaStock, 7 (eagle), Harry Collins Photography, 20, JaySi, 10, Kerimili, 1, 28, Kongkham35Gmail.com, 5, Konstantin Novikov, 24, LeonP, 7 (shark), Levent Konuk, 7 (clown fish), Mrinal Pal, cover (bottom right), pets in frames, 7 (tarantula), Ralph Eshelman, 21, Rostislav Stefanek, 18, TheLazyPineapple, cover (middle left), thka, 9 (top), Veronika 7833, 9 (bottom), Victor Shova, cover (top), Villiers Steyn, 12, wildestanimal, 19, worldwildlifewonders, 23, yanikap, 26

Artistic elements: Shutterstock/balabolka

Editorial Credits
Editor: Erika L. Shores; Designers: Dina Her and Juliette Peters; Media Researchers: Eric Gohl and Kelly Garvin; Production Specialist: Tori Abraham

TABLE OF CONTENTS

Words in **bold** are in the glossary.

INVESTIGATION: HOW DO WE GROUP?

Your clean clothes are mixed up in a basket. Look at the characteristics or features. What is the same? What is different? Put clothes with the same characteristics in the same place. They will be easier to find. Shirts in one drawer. Socks in another. Pants in the closet. You just grouped the clothes!

The same thing happens at zoos. Zookeepers understand the characteristics of different animals. Then they build **habitats**. The animals get grouped!

Now let's do a grouping activity. Look at the animals on page 7. Make **observations**. Think about the characteristics or features. In science these are **traits**. Do the animals have legs? Do they have feathers? Do they have fur?

Think about what is the same. Think about what is different. How would you group these animals?

Take a piece of paper. Write the animal names. Then group the animals. List traits that are the same.

ant   **butterfly**   **clownfish**   **deer**

eagle   **frog**   **peacock**   **polar bear**

salamander   **sea star**   **shark**   **snake**

spider   **turtle**

WHY DO SCIENTISTS GROUP ANIMALS?

Scientists can name and describe more than 1 million **species** of animals. That's a lot of animals!

Animals are part of our daily lives. Some animals are pets. Some animals live in our backyards. Some animals **pollinate** plants. These animals help humans. Other animals like ticks are **parasites**. They can cause humans problems. With so many animals in the world, why do scientists group them?

Remember how sorted animals help people find them in a zoo? Fish live with fish. Otters live with otters. Bats live with bats. Imagine if zookeepers had 1 million animals in a zoo!

Scientists put animals into groups
so that it is easier to learn about them.
Scientists can keep track of all the
ways animals are alike and different.

HOW DO SCIENTISTS GROUP ANIMALS?

All animals are put into two main groups. Animals with backbones, or spines, make up one group. They are **vertebrates**. Animals without backbones make up the second group. They are **invertebrates**.

Vertebrates are sorted into classes. The biggest classes are amphibians, reptiles, birds, fish, and mammals.

A lion is a vertebrate.

Invertebrates are sorted into many groups called **phyla**. The phylum with the most invertebrates are **arthropods**.

Think about your investigation. Did you group vertebrates and invertebrates?

A spider is an invertebrate.

WHICH ANIMALS ARE VERTEBRATES?

Have you ever seen a frog jump by a pond? Frogs are amphibians. Salamanders are too. Amphibians are cold-blooded. Their body temperature changes with the temperature of their surroundings. They breathe through their moist skin. They lay eggs. They live on land and in the water.

salamander

poison dart frog

Amphibians can be almost any color! Some really stand out, though. They are bright blue, green, and red. They can be poisonous. Poison dart frogs are the most poisonous animal in the world.

python

A snake slithers in the woods. Snakes are reptiles without legs. Other reptiles, like alligators and lizards, have legs. Turtles have legs and a shell.

Reptiles are cold-blooded like amphibians. But their skin is covered with scales or plates. They breathe with lungs. Most reptiles lay eggs. Some live on land. Some live in water.

The longest reptiles are python snakes and saltwater crocodiles. They can grow more than 20 feet (6 meters) long!

saltwater crocodile

Think about a fish in a lake. A fish is a swimming vertebrate. Fish have **gills** to breathe. They have scales and fins. They are cold-blooded like reptiles and amphibians.

Some fish live in freshwater. Trout and carp live in lakes and rivers. Other fish live in saltwater. Clownfish and snapper live in oceans.

trout

shark

Sharks and stingrays are also fish. But they don't have a full bony skeleton. Sharks and stingrays are in a small class of vertebrates. They have skeletons of **cartilage**.

falcon

Look up in the sky. See a bird? It's a flying vertebrate! All birds have feathers and wings. But not all birds fly. Ostriches can't fly. But they run fast. Penguins don't fly. But they swim fast.

All birds have beaks or bills. Birds also lay eggs. Birds are warm-blooded. Warm-blooded animals keep the inside of their bodies the same temperature all the time.

A penguin with egg and chick

The last group of vertebrates are mammals. Look in the mirror. You're a mammal! Mammals have hair or fur. Like birds, they are warm-blooded. Most have live babies. The babies drink the mother's milk.

Mammals breathe air. Mammals that live in water still need air. Whales and dolphins live in the water but come up to breathe.

dolphins

platypus

Sometimes mammals look like other vertebrates. A bat is a flying mammal. A platypus is a mammal that looks like a duck. It even lays eggs!

WHICH ANIMALS ARE INVERTEBRATES?

Scientists also group animals without backbones. They are called invertebrates. They are the largest group of animals. Imagine a pie chart made of animals. Almost all of the pie chart would be invertebrates!

squid

mite

You need a microscope to see the smallest invertebrate. It is called a mite. The biggest invertebrate has eyes the size of basketballs! It is a giant squid.

dragonfly

Sit outside. The largest group of invertebrates will keep you company. They are arthropods.

Insects are the largest group of arthropods. They have six legs. There are flying ones like butterflies and dragonflies. There are biting ones like mosquitoes. There are working ones like bees.

Other arthropods have more than six legs. Spiders and scorpions have eight legs. Crabs and lobsters have 10 legs. Millipedes have as many as 750 legs!

scorpion

Like vertebrates, invertebrates are grouped based on their traits. They are also grouped on their bodies and life cycles. Invertebrates include ocean animals like jellyfish and coral. Snails, clams, and octopi are grouped together. Sea stars and sand dollars are in another group.

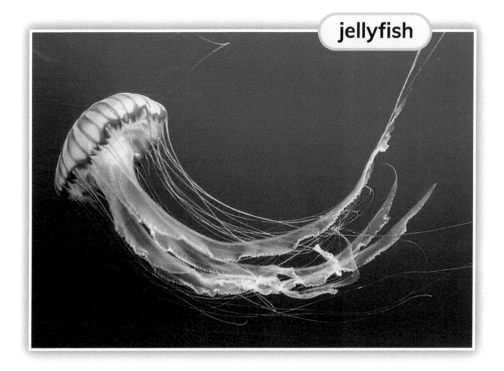

jellyfish

sea stars

There are so many animals in the world. It is easier for scientists to name and teach us about grouped animals. Scientists can also study and understand them better in groups.

Look back at your investigation. Would you change any of your groupings? Keep investigating!

GLOSSARY

arthropod (ar-THRO-pod)—an invertebrate with a segmented body and jointed legs

cartilage (KART-i-lig)—bendy, flexible tissue in animals

gill (GIL)—an organ on a fish to breathe

habitat (HAB-uh-tat)—the place where a plant or animal lives

invertebrate (in-VUR-tuh-bruht)—an animal without a backbone

observation (ob-zur-VAY-shuhn)—something that you have noticed by watching carefully

phyla (FI-la)—plural of phylum, a class of organisms

pollinate (POL-uh-nayt)—to take pollen from a flower to another flower

species (SPEE-sheez)—a group of animals or plants with common characteristics or features

trait (TRATE)—a characteristic or feature

vertebrate (VUR-tuh-bruht)—an animal with a backbone

READ MORE

Ferguson, Melissa. *Invertebrates: A 4D Book.* North Mankato, MN: Capstone Press, 2019.

Kalman, Bobbie. *What Kind of Animal Is It?* New York: Crabtree Publishing, 2018.

Mikoley, Kate. *What Are Animals?* New York: Gareth Stevens Publishing, 2020.

INTERNET SITES

Freshwater Fish of America
fws.gov/fisheries/freshwater-fish-of-america.html

Invertebrates
nationalgeographic.com/animals/invertebrates/

Vertebrates
ducksters.com/animals/vertebrates.php

INDEX